STUDY GUIDE

Understanding and Delighting in Your Differences

Men Are Like Waffles Women Are Like Spaghetti

BILL & PAM FARREL

HARVEST HOUSE PUBLISHERS
Eugene, Oregon 97402

Cover by Left Coast Design, Portland, Oregon

Published in association with the literary agency of Alive Communications, Inc., 7680 Goddard Street, Suite 200, Colorado Springs, CO 80920

MEN ARE LIKE WAFFLES—WOMEN ARE LIKE SPAGHETTI STUDY GUIDE
Copyright © 2002 by Bill and Pam Farrel
Published by Harvest House Publishers
Eugene, Oregon 97402

ISBN 0-7369-0878-1

Printed in the United States of America

02 03 04 05 06 07 / DP-MS / 10 9 8 7 6 5 4 3 2 1

Contents

Ingredients for a Great Marriage

*M*en *Are Like Waffles—Women Are Like Spaghetti* is a rather weird title for some very real truths and extremely practical principles—principles for relationships that really do work! And this should be no surprise, because the Author of all relationships created the principles and then wrote them in a love letter to us called the Bible. Within the pages of this study guide you will find a journey to deepen and strengthen your relationship by naturally integrating these principles into your love life. Each day's menu contains a few simple activities, and these work in conjunction with a once-a-week date night for the "Couple Communication Questions" found in the back of our book *Men Are Like Waffles—Women Are Like Spaghetti.*

As a couple, decide the best time for you to read the daily verses and have the table talk and prayer time (you will need five to fifteen minutes for this part). Either at this same time or later in the day, each of you can journal out your feelings about the day's topic. To begin, you will each need your Bible and your own study guide. (If you really like to put your thoughts down in writing, you may also wish to have a separate journal.) Then choose a date night time that is at least 30 minutes long, but preferably longer. We recommend three hours so that you have time for a meal together, a great discussion, and the extracurricular activities that might occur as your love life blossoms!

Connect the date night questions with some fun romantic date ideas (check pages 84-86 in *Men Are Like Waffles—Women Are Like Spaghetti* for inspiration.)

Here's a brief description of each marriage-building activity in the study guide:

The Daily Special

Each day, key verses are introduced that correspond to the topic. Following the verses are practical discussion questions to be talked over with your spouse.

Table Talk

We recommend that you set a time each day to discuss the day's topic. You might want to have a quick bite of breakfast together and then enjoy the guide as a quiet time/devotional aid. For other couples, after dinner or perhaps at bedtime might be more advantageous.

Prayer for the Day

Each day after the table talk you will find a prayer you can pray either with one another or on your own. Feel free to pray this prayer word for word, or adapt it and personalize it. The principle of praying together daily will bring strength to your relationship. In over 20 years of working with couples, we have *never* seen a couple divorce who have been committed to pray together daily.

Journal Assignment

Each day there will be a question for you to journal about. We have discovered that writing out prayers to Jesus and journaling out your feelings are safety valves for your relationship. Each of you should have your own journal so that your thoughts and feelings can remain private, although you are free to voluntarily share anything you wish. Often, if you write out your feelings before you verbally share them, God will shed new light on the situation. You might discover that something you thought was a fault of your spouse might actually be a shortcoming of yours. Or perhaps you will gain new insight into your spouse that will open you up to compassion or a plan on how to best approach your mate with an issue.

When I (Pam) journal, I first pray and ask God to lead me as I write. Then I reread the Scripture for the day and ask: "Is there a command to obey? A principle to observe? A sin to confess? A praise to give?" In other words, what does God want me to *do* as a result of reading this section of Scripture? Then after I write my thoughts I reread them and ask, "What have I learned?"

When I (Bill) journal, I ask God to slow me down enough to think about what is really going on in my life. I read the Scripture for the day and I pray: *God, help me think clearly today. Give me the insight I need to function well in my marriage today. You know exactly what I need to learn in order to function at my best, so please speak to my heart and help me be open to what will make me my best today.* I then write out the thoughts that come to mind in response to the verses I have read and the questions for the day.

In the journal section, you can answer the prompt given, journal out your feelings or thoughts, or simply record what you learned or how you will apply the verse(s) for the day.

Letter to My Love

At the end of each week you will write a letter to your spouse telling him/her what you have learned about yourself and your relationship. We will encourage creativity in this step through letters, poems, songs, pictures, and so on. Once a week, we encourage you to have a date night and take a copy of this love letter with you on the date. There is power in hearing, then receiving, words of love and affirmation. When the letter is read again, your spouse can hear your voice in each word you've written. Don't be concerned that you have to be some grand poet or write a long letter. It is the sincerity of your heart that is more important than the technique you use. Though there will be writing prompts, feel free to completely ignore them and just write whatever you want! This is your golden opportunity each week to share your heart, and however you decide to share is good. Let us give you a word of caution. This portion of the study guide can be a great place to give encouragement as your positive, loving words are read over and over again. But because the written word is so powerful, it may be the *worst* place to share negative feelings. You won't want these words read over and over, each time wounding your mate again. An overall principle that has served Bill and me well in our over 22 years together is to write out our feelings, pray over them privately, and then *verbally* share anything that is negative. As we share, we tread slowly and cautiously, being careful to read body language and facial expressions with the goal of speaking the truth in love (Ephesians 4:15).

As we said above, this date night is also a wonderful opportunity to do the "Couple Communication Questions" in the back of our book *Men Are Like Waffles—Women Are Like Spaghetti*. Your once-a-week date night can become a light at the end of the tunnel. Each week, the goal of date night is to connect romantically. The communication questions and the sharing of love letters is a wonderful way to layer love into your life. By creating this positive foundation weekly, tough issues become easier to tackle because there is an atmosphere of security and love in your relationship.

Overall, the best way to a better marriage is to become a better partner. The best way to become a better partner is to become a better person. While this study guide will deepen and strengthen your love, it will also strengthen and equip you as an individual. Your faith in God will grow, and from that reservoir you will gain the ability to be a conduit of God's love toward your spouse. As you embark on this fun adventure of love, enjoy your time together!

Week One

The Preparation of Waffles and Spaghetti

You know it's time for a marriage retreat when . . .

- ❧ She sets the table, and you're the only one who gets a paper plate.

- ❧ Lately, the family dog has been getting better cuts of meat than you.

- ❧ All week long she's only been making her side of the bed.

- ❧ Life is so stressful at your house, you've been in the bathtub since August.

- ❧ Your picture in his wallet has been replaced by a Kroger's discount card.

- ❧ The last night out he planned involved the Laundromat.

- ❧ With all your fighting, more flying objects can be seen in your house than at Roswell.

◈ You catch yourself trying to figure out a way to drop the kids off at church for summer Vacation Bible School and pick them up after the Christmas pageant.

◈ The last picnic lunch you shared was some crackers and Cheese Whiz you found under the front seat when the car broke down.[1]

This may be how you're feeling—or maybe you want to avoid feeling this way about your marriage. Either way, it's time for a retreat, and that's just what this study guide is meant to be—a short oasis each day to connect your hearts. If you're willing to take a few minutes each day and invest them well, you'll find love is a picnic—and not one featuring old Cheese Whiz from under the car seat! Let's focus this week on how God created us to be unique.

Day 1
The Daily Special

Then God said, "Let us make man in our image, in our likeness, and let them rule over the fish of the sea and the birds of the air, over the livestock, over all the earth, and over all the creatures that move along the ground." So God created man in his own image, in the image of God he created him; male and female he created them. God blessed them and said to them, "Be fruitful and increase in number; fill the earth and subdue it. Rule over the fish of the sea and the birds of the air and over every living creature that moves on the ground."   —Genesis 1:26-28

Table Talk

Three times in three verses, the Bible states that men and women are created in the image of God. What do you think this means? How does knowing that your spouse is made in God's image help you value him/her? When, in marriage, might holding your partner in high esteem as a creation of God help you as a couple? (In decision making? In conflict management? In deciding how to treat one another?)

Being created in the image of God does not mean we are exactly alike. In fact, God has made you very different than your spouse. In our book we say men are like waffles, women are like spaghetti, and we see that God created those differences to work *for* us in marriage. Compliment your spouse on at least one difference he/she has from you, and tell him/her why you think that difference is beneficial to your marriage and family.

Prayer for the Day

Lord, thank you for creating my spouse. You made him/her exactly what I needed to complement me. Lord, today help me see many ways in which my spouse reflects your image. Help me value my mate as a gift. Let me value my mate with the same kind of sacrificing love as you portrayed when you died for us on the cross. Amen.

Journal Assignment

List as many differences as you can think of in how you and your spouse think, act, and process life. Then write next to each difference how your marriage and/or family *benefits*. Choose one difference, and compliment your spouse all day, or even the rest of the week, whenever you see that difference enhancing your life.

_____

_____

_____

_____

_____

_____

_____

_____

_____

_____

_____

_____

_____

_____

Day 2
The Daily Special

The Lord God said, "It is not good for the man to be alone. I will make a helper suitable for him."

—Genesis 2:18

Read also Genesis 2:19-25 in your Bible.

Table Talk

God designed marriage to be a blessed union between a husband and wife. If you are newlyweds, think of some couples you know who have healthy marriages. What are some of the habits they have in their marriage? (If you don't know, call them up for a coffee double date and ask!) For example, a habit we have had in our relationship since engagement is that we pray before each meal then kiss. It is hard to stay mad at someone you kiss that often! If you have been married awhile, what habits are you glad you have layered into your life? Are there any habits, behaviors, or actions you used to have in your marriage, maybe during courtship or your first few years together, that you'd like to see return? Talk about how to integrate those healthy habits back into your relationship.

Prayer for the Day

God, thank you for the model of a healthy marriage. Today help me value my spouse as my best friend, the one who completes me. Help us show respect to one another and keep our relationship a priority. Amen.

Journal Assignment

Which part of the foundation of your marriage is the weakest? Look at the list below and choose one area. Brainstorm ways *you* (not your spouse) can help strengthen that area. Commit to one idea. Write out your commitment as a prayer to God.

❧ *Companionship.* How's your friendship?

❧ *Completeness.* Are you valuing your spouse's strengths?

❧ *Connection.* Are you respecting your mate's opinions, decision-making style, parenting, etc.? Are you looking for ways to help him/her become his/her God-given best?

❧ *Cleaving.* Are you treating your marriage relationship as a priority over parents, extended family, work, and other friendships?

❧ *Closeness.* Is your sex life active and consistent? Are you interested in your spouse's needs as much as your own? Does your sexual interaction give evidence that the rest of your relationship is healthy?

_____

_____

_____

_____

_____

_____

Day 3
The Daily Special

The LORD God commanded the man, "You are free to eat from any tree in the garden; but you must not eat from the tree of the knowledge of good and evil, for when you eat of it you will surely die."

The LORD God said, "It is not good for the man to be alone. I will make a helper suitable for him."

—Genesis 2:16-18

Now the serpent was more crafty than any of the wild animals the LORD God had made. He said to the woman, "Did God really say, 'You must not eat from any tree in the garden'?"

The woman said to the serpent, "We may eat fruit from the trees in the garden, but God did say, 'You must not eat fruit from the tree that is in the middle of the garden, and you must not touch it, or you will die.'"

—Genesis 3:1-3

Table Talk

Today's verses are in two parts. The first section explains God's command to Adam:

"You are free to eat from any tree in the garden; but you must not eat from the tree of the knowledge of good and evil, for when you eat of it you will surely die."

Then in chapter 3, we see Eve's rendition:

"We may eat fruit from the trees in the garden, but God did say, 'You must not eat fruit from the tree that is in the middle of the garden, and you must not touch it, or you will die.'"

Notice the difference?

Eve added, "If you touch it, you will die." We don't know for sure if God told Eve the parameters or if Adam did. We're not sure if Eve was half listening and got it wrong or if she thought, "I'll just add to it, and if I don't touch it, I won't eat it!" (Not a bad idea if she'd followed it—but it wasn't what God said!)

Adam and Eve had different reads on the same command. How well do you really communicate? Do you give your mate enough details so you both are on the same page?

Rate your disclosure on the chart below:

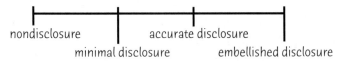

When are you most likely to not be accurate (either less than the full truth or embellishing the truth)? Why do you think you are making those choices (fear of spouse's wrath, disapproval, pain from past)? Talk with each other about the balance between truth and tact.

An entry statement can help you when you are trying to share the truth in a difficult area. One of Bill's entry statements is, "Pam, I have something I need to talk to you about, but it may be hard to hear." When Bill uses this statement, I try not to overreact no matter what he might say. As he is sharing with me, I try to place myself in his shoes, and that helps me listen better and with less volatile emotion. This frees Bill to share more fully.

Try to come up with your own entry statements that will enable you to speak honestly, and with love, to one another.

Prayer for the Day

*Lord, help us both to be honest and accurate as we
share with one another. More importantly, let us both
be honest and accurate in our relationship with you.
Help us rightly divide your Word and accurately share
it, teach it, and apply it to our lives today. Amen.*

Journal Assignment

Eve made up her own version of the truth. When are you
most tempted to do that? Eve may have added to God's command out of fear. Have you added rules to your life, your marriage, your worship, or your children's lives that are based in fear?
(For example, your wife can't have friends without your
approval; your kids can't do anything without one of you present, no matter what age they are; your schedule is inflexible;
your husband has no freedom to spend time with his friends;
you have become legalistic in your church involvement.) God's
Word says, "Perfect love casts out fear." Write out a statement
that describes how God's perfect love can help you live in truth.

_____

_____

_____

_____

_____

_____

_____

_____

Day 4
The Daily Special

Then the man and his wife heard the sound of the
LORD God as he was walking in the garden in the cool
of the day, and they hid from the LORD God among
the trees of the garden. But the LORD God called to
the man, "Where are you?"
—Genesis 3:8,9

Read the context of these verses in Genesis 3:4-13.

Table Talk

How do you handle it when you sin? Do you cop out
and blame your spouse the way Adam did? Adam and
Eve entered into sin together and reaped grave consequences. Have you and your mate a history of sin-
ning together? For example, maybe where you met
one another isn't a place you're proud of. Or perhaps
your early choices weren't God's best.

The best way to safeguard your marriage is to
come clean before God together. If you need to, pray
the repentance prayer below:

*Lord, you tell us if we confess our sins, you will be faithful
and just to forgive our sins and cleanse us from all unright-
eousness. We now confess that as a couple we _____*

_____.

*Please wash us and we will be whiter than snow. We want a
fresh start and clean hearts before you. Amen.*

Prayer for the Day

Make Psalm 25:4-7 your prayer for today:

> *Show me your ways, O LORD, teach me your paths;*
> *guide me in your truth and teach me, for you are God*
> *my Savior, and my hope is in you all day long.*
> *Remember, O LORD, your great mercy and love, for they*
> *are from of old. Remember not the sins of my youth and*
> *my rebellious ways; according to your love remember*
> *me, for you are good, O LORD.*

Journal Assignment

Two of the elements that keep relationships fresh are repentance and growth. What areas in your lives were hurt or damaged by past choices? What steps can you as an individual take to rebuild in the areas that might have been impacted by poor choices in the past? What area of your marriage do you think needs more work, more information, more steps of growth? What can you do as an individual to grow in that area?

_____

_____

_____

_____

_____

_____

_____

Day 5
The Daily Special

The LORD God said, "The man has now become like one of us, knowing good and evil. He must not be allowed to reach out his hand and take also from the tree of life and eat, and live forever." So the LORD God banished him from the Garden of Eden to work the ground from which he had been taken.

—Genesis 3:22,23

Read the context of these verses in Genesis 3:14–4:1.

Table Talk

The consequences for breaking God's plans are sometimes painful! What adversity have you been through as a couple? What did you do right to help get you through the struggle? What do you wish you had done differently? What transitions are ahead for you that might be sources of turmoil? What can you do as a couple to prepare for adversity?

Prayer for the Day

Lord, help us to be strong and courageous, knowing that you are with us wherever we go. We know that our life will not be perfect. We will experience setbacks and frustrations. Help us increase in strength in the midst of the struggles and teach us how to encourage one another when life gets hard. Thank you for putting us together as teammates for the journey of life. Amen.

Journal Assignment

Animals had to be sacrificed to cover Adam and Eve after they sinned. Sin always exacts a toll. Think back over your life together. What sin(s) forced a sacrifice to be paid by someone you love? For example, if one of you had an addictive behavior, the other spouse may have sacrificed time, money, and energy. Once my mother (Pam's) added up how much money my father had spent on alcohol and cigarettes over the course of their marriage. It was more than enough money to send all three of us children to Ivy League schools! Is your family making an undue, unnecessary sacrifice for any of your behaviors? (Do the kids have to hide out when you experience PMS? Does your wife have to clear the company out because of your anger?) Ask God to show you if any of your behaviors, actions, or attitudes are causing your family to pay a high price. What changes do you need to make?

_____

_____

_____

_____

_____

_____

_____

_____

_____

Letter to My Love

What did you learn this week that changed your heart toward your spouse? Write him/her a letter and give the gift of support and encouragement. (Options: Consider all the ways your mate is different from you. Create a poem, a song, or even a list that shows how those differences are a gift to your heart, soul, and life.)

Week Two

Waffles and Spaghetti Communicating

Communicating can be difficult between genders. Consider this dictionary for women as a help:

Argument (ar*gyou*ment) n
A discussion that occurs when you're right, but he just hasn't realized it yet.

Balance the checkbook (bal*ens da chek*buk) v
To go to the cash machine and hit "inquire."

Bar-be-que (bar*bi*q) n
You bought the groceries, washed the lettuce, chopped the tomatoes, diced the onions, marinated the meat, and cleaned everything up, but *he* "made the dinner."

Eternity (e*ter*ni*tee) n
The last two minutes of a basketball game.

Hardware Store (hard*war stor) n

Similar to a black hole in space—if he goes in, he isn't coming out anytime soon.[1]

The best dictionary for love is one another. This week's activities should help build a bit of understanding.

Day 1
The Daily Special

Set a guard over my mouth, O LORD; keep watch over
the door of my lips.   —Psalm 141:3

Read also Proverbs 11:12; Proverbs 16:1; Proverbs 21:33; Proverbs 13:3; and James 1:26.

Table Talk

In speech, often "less is best." Chances are you had a mother who said, "If you can't say something nice, don't say anything at all." My (Pam's) mother used to say, "If in doubt, don't."

And in conversation, this principle has served me well. When I am doubting whether or not I should say something, I probably shouldn't say it—and when I have gone ahead and said it anyway, most of the time I have been sorry I said it.

Because Bill and I work with so many couples in conflict, we hear some very cruel and awful things people have said to one another outside our office. Some are so hurtful and mean no person should ever have to hear them. If you are very angry, it is much better to buy yourself some time than to emotionally explode on your spouse. You can choose to say things like, "I am just not ready to talk yet. Can we reschedule to tonight?" (or sometime later that you feel you will be prepared to talk with words that have been weighed out). Another option is, "I don't want either of us to say anything we'll regret. Why don't we take a break and pray through this issue, then come back and see if God has given us some new insights?" One phrase Bill and I use often is, "Can we pray instead of fight?"

Today, talk about how you know when you ought *not* to speak. I (Pam) feel a check from the Holy Spirit, a kind of whisper to my soul, that grows louder in my heart as I argue with God when I want to speak during times he wants me to be quiet. Also answer this question, "How do I decide what not to say when I *do* get to speak?"

Prayer for the Day

Lord, set a guard on my lips. Let me weigh my words with you before I speak. Give me words to speak to all those I love that are the words you have chosen for them to hear. Amen.

Journal Assignment

From today's verses, what are the results of NOT guarding your words? Have you said some things recently that you are sure have hurt another, or are untrue, ungracious, ungrateful, irreverent, or just unnecessary? Do you have any pet sayings that are unwholesome or unkind? (Like "Hey, woman, get me that…" or "My old lady…" or "My old man…") Why do you think you say hurtful things? Today, look at your words, figure out why you say some of the ones that hurt, and then ask God to be your protection rather than using hurtful words to protect your heart.

_____

_____

_____

_____

_____

_____

_____

_____

_____

_____

_____

Day 2
The Daily Special

Put away perversity from your mouth; keep corrupt talk far from your lips.   —Proverbs 4:24

Read also Proverbs 10:32; Ephesians 5:4; and James 3:9-12.

Table Talk

Look at the verses on page 28. What kind of things do we *know* God doesn't want us to say? Create a personal working definition of the terms below.

Perversity:

Corrupt talk:

Obscenity:

Foolish Talk:

Coarse joking:

Cursing:

When are you most likely to use any of the above kind of language? Is it when you feel backed into a corner, or is it just a habit? To break a bad habit, you can't just say, "I won't say that." Instead, *choose* what to say instead. Choose one phrase that you'd like out of your vocabulary and put in its place a new phrase that is more positive or encouraging.

Prayer for the Day

Lord, today, help me say only what is fitting. Help me choose words of thanksgiving and praise. God, help me replace my talk with your talk. Help me develop a habit of saying what is good and right and what will give grace to people and glory to you. Amen.

Journal Assignment

Many of us have avoided the habit of swearing and coarse language, but some of us still have language that harms rather than helps. In the front of one of the books Bill and I were given on our wedding day, a note was inscribed by a couple who had been married several decades: "Take sarcasm out of your relationship." Do you have words or phrases you use that cut your spouse? Do you criticize him/her regularly? Do you criticize your mate in front of others? Do you use jokes to get your point across, then tag on the line, "Just kidding"? Replace your negative speech with some positive words. Philippians 4:8 says, "Finally, brothers, whatever is true, whatever is noble, whatever is right, whatever is pure, whatever is lovely, whatever is admirable—if anything is excellent or praiseworthy—think about such things." Think of some nice things to say about your spouse. What is true and noble about him/her? What is right and pure about him/her? What is lovely or admirable? What is excellent or praiseworthy? Write out some positive things to say today.

_____

_____

_____

_____

_____

_____

_____

_____

_____

_____

Day 3
The Daily Special

My mouth speaks what is true, for my lips detest wickedness. All the words of my mouth are just; none of them is crooked or perverse. —Proverbs 8:7,8

Read also Proverbs 6:16-19; Proverbs 15:4; Proverbs 16:13; and Proverbs 24:26.

Table Talk

The solid base of a relationship is honesty. When a mate deceives in big or small ways, the foundation and strength of the relationship are compromised. Acts of deception are always harmful to a relationship.

On the other hand, brutal honesty is just that— brutal. If your spouse asks, "Do I look fat in this?" and you answer, "Yes," you might find yourself sleeping on the sofa! (Keep in mind that some questions are better never asked!) Tact is the ability to speak the truth in love (Ephesians 4:15). Today, each of you answer this question, "How can I tell you the truth and not hurt your feelings?" One of my (Pam's) favorite principles from God's Word is John 8:32, which says, "Then you will know the truth, and the truth will set you free."

Remember your entry statements from last week? Review them and also brainstorm some other phrases you each can use when you need to share the truth in love. For example, "I have some healing words," or "I have some truth to set you free." Each of you share a few phrases and then ask your spouse which is the easiest for them to hear and which will best prepare their heart for a hard conversation.

Prayer for the Day

Lord, help us today to speak truth and healing into each other's hearts. Keep us from deceptions, large or small. God, help me value the truth when it is spoken. And let me always speak the truth in love. Amen.

Journal Assignment

1 Corinthians 16:14 says, "Do everything in love." Honesty is love in action. How honest are you? Are you spending money your spouse isn't aware of? Are you spending time with people that you aren't letting your mate know about? Would you be willing to let your spouse know how you spend *all* your time?

Try to look at your life from God's point of view. Would he say you are living an honest life? Before you can be honest with your mate, you need to be honest before God. King David tried to live out a deception that included a murder, an affair, and a cover up, but he was still called "a man after God's own heart." Could it be because he came clean? Read David's prayer to God in Psalm 51 and then write out your own prayer of confession and repentance. You might simply start it, "I'm sorry, God . . ."

_____

_____

_____

_____

_____

_____

Day 4
The Daily Special

A gentle answer turns away wrath, but a harsh word stirs up anger.   —Proverbs 15:1

Read also Proverbs 8:6; Proverbs 16:24; Ephesians 4:29; and 1 Thessalonians 5:11.

Table Talk
After reading today's verses, what kind of words should be a priority to communicate? Ask your mate what he/she has to face today that they may not be looking forward to. Build up your spouse and give an encouraging word that will help prepare the one you love for the journey ahead for him/her today.

Prayer for the Day
Lord, today let the words of my mouth be pleasant like a honeycomb; sweet and healing to the soul. Let my words be worthy and gentle, and let them be words that build up others. Amen.

Journal Assignment
God commands us to speak words that build up others. In what areas is your mate discouraged or insecure? Write out a set of encouraging words and seek to partner with God to build them up in this area.

_____

_____

_____

_____

_____

_____

_____

_____

_____

_____

Day 5
The Daily Special

My dear brothers, take note of this: Everyone should be quick to listen, slow to speak and slow to become angry.

—James 1:19

Table Talk

Be sure you have read chapter 2 in *Men Are Like Waffles—Women Are Like Spaghetti*. Most of this chapter on communication focuses on being a good listener. What did you learn about listening? What listening skill would you like to work on today? Start right now by listening to your mate as he/she completes this sentence: "I can tell you are listening to me, really listening to me, when you _____."

(For example, "You put things down and turn to me."

Or, "You turn the TV off and come close and touch me.")

Prayer for the Day

Lord, give me a listening heart. Calm the frantic pace and distractions of my life so I can hear what is really important to my mate. Help me be quick to listen and slow to speak. Amen.

Journal Assignment

Often, the reason we aren't good listeners is because we are preoccupied with our own problems or concerns. Make a list of the concerns that are weighing you down, and then write a prayer committing them to God's care. Anytime today that you are listening to your spouse and you notice the preoccupations start to creep back in, pray, "They are yours, God. Give me a listening heart." Then refocus on your mate.

_____

_____

_____

_____

_____

_____

_____

_____

_____

Letter to My Love

Write a letter to your love. Complete this sentence:

Honey, I have learned the most incredible things about you as I have listened to you lately. What I remember most is…

Week Three
Waffles and Spaghetti Relaxing

Men's advice for women:

❖ If we're in the backyard and the TV in the den is on, that doesn't mean we're not watching it.

❖ Don't tell anyone we can't afford a new car. Tell them we don't want one.

❖ Only wearing your new lingerie once does not send the message that you need more. It tells us lingerie is a bad investment.

❖ Please don't drive when you're not driving.

❖ Don't feel compelled to tell us how all the people in your little stories are related to one another. We're just nodding, waiting for the punch line.

❖ The quarterback who just got pummeled isn't trying to be brave, he's just not crying. Big difference.

❖ When the waiter asks if everything's okay, a simple "Yes" will do.

❖ When I'm turning the wheel and the car is nosing onto the off-ramp, saying "This is our exit" is not strictly necessary.

❖ SportsCenter starts at 11:00 P.M. and runs one hour. This is an excellent time for you to pay bills, put laundry in the dryer, or talk to your sister.

❖ Two hot dogs and a soda at a baseball game do, in fact, constitute going out to dinner.

❖ It's in neither your interest nor ours to take the *Cosmo* quiz together.

❖ No, you can't have the remote control.[1]

Remote controls or remote places—each gender has a pattern to their relaxation, and they take it very seriously! This week's exercises will help you find a way to snuggle up together.

Day 1
The Daily Special

Six days you shall labor, but on the seventh day you shall rest; even during the plowing season and harvest you must rest.
                                        —Exodus 34:21

Table Talk

God created for six straight days, and then on the seventh he rested. Each year in Israel there were approximately 70 days of festivals. Between the Sabbaths and celebrations, the Israelites received approximately 120 days off a year. Then God set aside one year in seven for the land to rest. There was to be no planting or harvesting, so the farmers got the year off too. God built rest into the system because he knew we needed it. Take a moment to add up your total number of days off per year.

His:

Hers:

Then add up how many you have TOGETHER:

Now, on how many of those days off do you carry out other major responsibilities? Subtract these from the total. Do you have any time for rest left? Each of you comment on the above totals. Do you feel you have enough "down" time as a couple? Are your optional responsibilities on your days off ones that bring ful-fillment or a sense of purpose? Do they build into your family or future? Overall, are you satisfied with the big picture of the time off you have together? To keep the conversation from drifting into finances, each of you share your favorite free activity to do that brings you rest. (Sleeping in together is one of our favorites.)

Prayer for the Day
Lord, help us follow your example and remember to rest. Amen.

Journal Assignment
When Israel had time off, much of it was spent in celebration and praise for what the Lord had done for them. Write a prayer or psalm that thanks God for something in your life this past year.

_____

_____

_____

_____

_____

_____

_____

_____

_____

_____

_____

Day 2
The Daily Special

If a man has recently married, he must not be sent to war or have any other duty laid on him. For one year he is to be free to stay at home and bring happiness to the wife he has married.   —Deuteronomy 24:5

Table Talk

It's obvious God holds relationships in priority! List a few benefits of having less responsibility the first year of marriage. Having time to adjust to marriage, or having time to focus on building your marriage, is a choice—one that can reap very wonderful consequences. When Bill and I were newlyweds, we didn't own a television—the best decision we ever made! Instead of watching TV we talked, walked, ministered together—and had plenty of time to celebrate our love. As we had children, we each gave up other activities (Bill gave up golf, and I gave up shopping for fun) so we could have more time together. Is there something you can cut back on or take a sabbatical from for a season (you can discuss for how long) so you gain some additional time for one another?

Prayer for the Day

Dear God, help us see each other as a life priority. Amen.

Journal Assignment

Selfishness is usually one of the things that stand in the way of couples having more time for one another. When you do have time together, selfishness can also be a roadblock when determining how that time will be spent. Examine your heart. Have you been selfish with your time lately? Write out three to four gifts of time you could give your spouse unselfishly. For example, a massage, letting him/her choose the restaurant on your next date, or not asking him to do your "honey do" list on his next day off. What gift of time do you think God wants you to give your mate? Write a commitment to God to give that gift below:

_____

_____

_____

_____

_____

_____

_____

_____

_____

_____

_____

_____

Day 3
The Daily Special

My soul finds rest in God alone; my salvation comes
from him.
                                        —Psalm 62:1

Also check out Jesus' thoughts on rest in Matthew 11:28-30.

Table Talk

In God's presence is rest. When do you receive rest
from worshiping God? On the day you attend
church? Everyday? Maybe just a few times a year?
How might you rest in God this week together? Perhaps you could listen to a concert or praise CD, or
maybe take a walk in nature. Talk about and then
choose an activity to do together this week that will
nourish your spirits.

Prayer for the Day

Lord, slow us down so that your presence may refresh us. Amen.

Journal Assignment

Jesus said to come to him when we are weary and "heavy laden" (Matthew 11:28 KJV). Write a letter to Jesus and tell him what is making you weary these days.

_____

_____

_____

_____

_____

_____

_____

_____

Day 4
The Daily Special

If you keep your feet from breaking the Sabbath and from doing as you please on my holy day, if you call the Sabbath a delight and the LORD's holy day honorable, and if you honor it by not going your own way and not doing as you please or speaking idle words, then you will find your joy in the LORD, and I will cause you to ride on the heights of the land and to feast on the inheritance of your father Jacob.

—Isaiah 58:13,14

Table Talk

Sundays have really changed over the years. It used to be businesses closed on Sundays. Blue laws prohibited the sale of alcohol on Sundays. Sundays were the day for family gatherings, big after-church meals, and naps. What traditions did your family have for Sundays when you were growing up? What traditions or activities, or "non-activities," would you like to incorporate into your day of worship?

Prayer for the Day

Lord, help us look at the Sabbath from your point of view, not ours. How do you want us to spend our Sundays? Our desire is to honor you. Amen.

Journal Assignment

Write out your favorite Sunday memory. What made it so special?

_____

_____

_____

_____

_____

_____

_____

Day 5
The Daily Special

One generation will commend your works to another;
they will tell of your mighty acts.   —Psalm 145:4

Read the context of this verse in Psalm 145:3-7.

Table Talk

What priorities are your children picking up from the way you are spending your Sundays? Do sports seem more important than relationships? Does the yard appear to be more worthy of attention than they are? Is the day filled with chores? Arguing? All fun and no worship? More is caught than taught—what are your kids catching as the priority on the Sabbath?

Prayer for the Day

God, show us how we can use your day to pass on the great things you have done for us to our children and our children's children. Amen.

Journal Assignment

You can't pass on what you don't possess. List as many great things as you can think of that you want to tell your children (or nieces, nephews, or grandchildren) that God has done for you.

_____

_____

_____

_____

_____

_____

_____

_____

_____

_____

_____

_____

_____

Letter to My Love

Write a letter to your spouse that shares the most precious Sabbath memories you have, why they were special, and what change you'd like to see happen so that more of your Sundays together (or another day of rest) could have some of those same elements.

Week Four

Waffles and Spaghetti in Love

When David and Kathy were approaching their fortieth anniversary, they decided they wanted to renew their wedding vows. As friends gathered together to discuss the details of the ceremony, Kathy started describing the dress she was planning to wear. Then one of her friends asked what color shoes she had to go with the dress.

Kathy replied, "Silver."

At that point her husband chimed in, "Yep, silver...to match her hair."

Shooting a look at David's head, Kathy's friend said, "So David, I guess you are going barefoot?"

Life is full of challenges, setbacks, and unwanted outcomes. At the same time, life is also full of great relationships and memories. To maximize the victories and overcome the setbacks, everybody needs encouragement. This week's focus is on encouraging the one you love.

Day 1
The Daily Special

> But encourage one another daily, as long as it is
> called Today, so that none of you may be hardened
> by sin's deceitfulness.
>   —Hebrews 3:13

Also look at the call to encouragement in 1 Thessalonians
5:11.

Table Talk

The word "encourage" is made up of two Greek
words—*para,* which means "alongside," and *kaleo,*
which means "to be called." The word literally means,
"called alongside to help." When you encourage your
spouse, you are committing yourself to be alongside
to help in whatever way you can. The amazing thing
about encouragement to us is that it is one of the
works of the Holy Spirit. In John 14:16, Jesus pointed
out to his disciples, "I will ask the Father, and he will
give you another Counselor to be with you forever."
The word "Counselor" in this verse is the Greek word
paraclete or "one who is called alongside." The Holy
Spirit is in our lives to encourage, and when you
encourage your spouse you are partnering with the
Holy Spirit in his work.

Take a minute and build up your spouse. Be
grateful for who he/she is and what he/she did for
you yesterday. Think back one day. What would you
like to thank your spouse for?

Prayer for the Day

Lord, let me not take my spouse for granted. Help me remember to affirm and encourage somehow, some way, every day. Amen.

Journal Assignment

It is easy to take for granted all the things your spouse may do for you. When was the last time you thanked him/her for doing the dishes or laundry or putting gas in the car? List eight to ten everyday things you can thank your spouse for. Now put on an attitude of gratitude and look for ways to say thanks creatively each day this week.

_____

_____

_____

_____

_____

_____

_____

_____

_____

_____

_____

_____

Day 2
The Daily Special

You hear, O LORD, the desire of the afflicted; you
encourage them, and you listen to their cry.

—Psalm 10:17

Table Talk

Give your spouse the gift of listening. Listen, without
comment, as your mate completes this statement:
"Lately, the thing that has made me feel like I want to
cry is _____."

(Feel free to hold, pray for, wipe tears—just do not
insert your opinion. Try listening for at least five
minutes.)

Prayer for the Day

*Lord, today help me hear the heart of my spouse. Let
his/her burden be lighter because of something I say or
do. Give me the ability to hear from you how you want
me to respond. Amen.*

Journal Assignment

A few of the marriages we've seen crumble came apart simply
because one of the partners didn't know how to handle the
other's emotions. Some want to run away and escape when emotions run too high, others want to try to make their spouse feel
stupid for having those feelings, and still others use those feelings
shared in vulnerability as a manipulative tool to maintain control over the relationship. How do you deal with the harder-to-

handle emotions of your spouse (feelings of depression, sadness, grief, anger, and frustration)? Which of your mate's emotions is the most challenging for you? Is there someone else in your mate's life that seems good at handling that emotion? (For example, my (Pam's) brother was great at handling my "drama queen" episodes. He always seemed to be able to make me laugh, and that would help my sadness lift. As Bill watched Bret relate to me, Bill gained some insights.) Write down which of your mate's emotions you want to gain a better response to so you can handle circumstances better when your mate is expressing that feeling.

_____

_____

_____

_____

_____

_____

_____

_____

_____

Day 3
The Daily Special

Do nothing out of selfish ambition or vain conceit, but in humility consider others better than your-selves.
—Philippians 2:3

Read the context of today's verse in Philippians 2:1-7.

Table Talk

"Do nothing from selfishness . . . consider others . . ." Each of you pick a day this week to defer to the other's wishes. Go to dinner where he/she chooses or say yes to an activity your mate wants to try. Give the one you love the gift of considering only him/her for an entire day.

Prayer for the Day

God, I am selfish. I acknowledge that I often want my own way. Lord, make me more like you—other-centered instead of so self-centered. Moment by moment, all day today, gently remind me when I am being selfish in any way, in any setting, with anyone. Amen.

Journal Assignment

Take a step back and look at all your interactions with people. When do you see that you are most prone to selfishness? (For example, when Bill and I are dead tired, we can be much more selfish.) What can you do to avoid selfishness? Will you choose to defer to the other person if in doing so it will be in that person's best interest?

_____

_____

_____

_____

_____

_____

_____

_____

_____

Day 4
The Daily Special

The islanders showed us unusual kindness. They built a fire and welcomed us all because it was raining and cold.
—Acts 28:2

Read also Colossians 3:12 and consider the "clothes" God wants you to wear.

After Paul landed in Malta, he said the islanders showed him "unusual kindness." Often Bill and I will look at each other after counseling a couple and ask, "Why can't people just be kind?"

Colossians 3:12 tells us that as God's people we should be clothed with kindness. That means we can "put on" kindness the way we'd pull a shirt out of the closet and put it on. We can choose to be kind at any time. Instead of saying something today that is encouraging, *do* something today that is kind. Be *unusually* kind.

Table Talk

Each of you think of a few times you have been delighted or surprised by another person's unusual kindness (someone other than your spouse). What did that person do that made the kindness so unusual?

Prayer for the Day

Father in heaven, help me be unusually kind to everyone I see today. Then tomorrow, help me be unusually kind, and the day after too. Help me to put on kindness so that it becomes a part of my nature. Amen.

Journal Assignment

As your spouse shared today, did you catch any glimpses of what he/she thinks is unusually kind? Did *unusually* kind mean someone went out of their way? Or perhaps helped him/her when he/she was in a tough spot? Was it a very personal gift or an elaborate expression of love? See if you can get your spouse to share several examples of unusual kindness, and as you do, see if there is a pattern you can follow so that you can be unusually kind to him/her this week.

_____

_____

_____

_____

_____

_____

Day 5
The Daily Special

Love is patient, love is kind. It does not envy, it does not boast, it is not proud. It is not rude, it is not self-seeking, it is not easily angered, it keeps no record of wrongs. Love does not delight in evil but rejoices

with the truth. It always protects, always trusts, always hopes, always perseveres. Love never fails....
—1 Corinthians 13:4-8

Table Talk

The way to a more loving relationship is to be more loving yourself! So let's take a look at what goes into love:

- ❖ patient = long passion, willing to wait
- ❖ kind = gentle in behavior
- ❖ does not envy = does not boil over relationships
- ❖ does not boast = does not play the part of the bragger
- ❖ not proud = does not puff oneself out like a pair of bellows
- ❖ not rude = not indecent
- ❖ not self-seeking = not seeking after its own interests
- ❖ not easily angered = is not easily irritated and avoids sharpness of spirit
- ❖ keeps no record of wrongs = does not record in a ledger book the bad things done
- ❖ does not delight in evil = finds no joy in the triumph of evil
- ❖ rejoices with the truth = finds joy in everything that is true
- ❖ protects = covers like a roof
- ❖ trusts = has faith in people without being gullible

- ◈ hopes = sees the bright side of things and does not despair
- ◈ perseveres = carries on like a stout-hearted soldier
- ◈ Love never fails = love survives everything

Compliment your spouse by telling him/her which of these definitions of love he/she does best. Give him/her an example of a time when you most appreciated that definition of love in your life. For example, I (Pam) appreciate Bill's patience, especially when I make a mistake. He never raises his voice at me, and he never swears or demeans me.

I (Bill) appreciate how much Pam rejoices in the truth. As she keeps taking her life back to the Word of God, she keeps growing and developing as a person. Her open heart for truth takes a lot of pressure off of our relationship.

Now, talk about the traits of love *you* most appreciate receiving from your mate from 1 Corinthians 13.

Prayer for the Day

Lord, today let me be more patient and kind. Help me not to be envious, boastful, or proud. Help me be less rude and not so self-seeking. Keep me from being easily angered and help me let go of wrongs suffered. Help me not delight in evil but rejoice with the truth. Help me protect and trust my love. Lord, give us both hope and a persevering love. Amen.

Journal Assignment

How are you doing on that love list? How patient are you? How kind? Look over the traits of love in this verse and rate yourself 1-10 (10 being perfection). Then go back and write a definition of that trait for your own life. For example: *Love is patient. I will be more forgiving when Bill runs late and when he can't get to tasks I thought were important.*

_____

_____

_____

_____

_____

_____

_____

_____

_____

_____

_____

_____

_____

_____

_____

_____

Letter to My Love

Write a letter of encouragement thanking your spouse for a time when he/she was *unusually* kind.

Week Five

Waffles and Spaghetti in the Bedroom

Whose Hands

A basketball in my hands is worth about $19.

A basketball in Michael Jordan's hands is worth about $33 million.

It depends on whose hands it's in.

A baseball in my hands is worth about $6.

A baseball in Mark McGwire's hands is worth about $19 million.

It depends on whose hands it's in.

A tennis racket is useless in my hands.

A tennis racket in Pete Sampras' hands is a Wimbledon Championship.

It depends on whose hands it's in.

A rod in my hands will keep away a wild animal.

A rod in Moses' hands will part the mighty sea.

It depends on whose hands it's in.

A slingshot in my hands is a kid's toy.
A slingshot in David's hand is a mighty weapon.
It depends on whose hands it's in.

Two fish and five loaves of bread in my hands is a couple of
    fish sandwiches.
Two fish and five loaves of bread in God's hands will feed
    thousands.
It depends on whose hands it's in.

Nails in my hands might produce a birdhouse.
Nails in Jesus Christ's hands will produce salvation for the
    entire world.
It depends on whose hands it's in.

As you see now it depends on whose hands it's in.

So put
your concerns,
your worries,
your fears,
your hopes,
your dreams,
your families, and
your relationships
in God's hands because—
It depends on whose hands it's in.[1]

The success of your sex life depends on whose hands it is in!
This week we'll look at the mystery of becoming "one flesh."

Day 1
The Daily Special

For this reason a man will leave his father and mother and be united to his wife, and they will become one flesh.

—Genesis 2:24

Read more about what God has to say regarding sexual intimacy in 1 Corinthians 7:3-5 and Hebrews 13:4.

Table Talk

When you were married, you agreed to allow your spouse to have "co-ownership" of your body. It is not that you gave up control of yourself, but you did enter into a sexual partnership so that your body does not belong to you alone but also belongs to your spouse. As a result, there is a responsibility to discover how your "other" body works and to help your spouse discover how your body works. Talk over the following questions with your spouse:

1. What sights, sounds, smells, and activities arouse your body?

2. How does sexual arousal feel in your body? Where does it start? How does it move through your body?

3. In the area of sexuality, what do you think is the best part of having the body you have?

4. In the area of sexuality, what is the hardest thing about having the body you have?

Prayer for the Day

Dear God, thank you for the body you have given me and for the body you have given my spouse. Help me to better understand the needs of my spouse's body. Please do something today to make my spouse feel handsome/beautiful. Thank you for creating sex as a gift for my spouse and me. Teach me ways to love my spouse that will make our sex life satisfying to both of us. Amen.

Journal Assignment

Grade yourself on how open you have been to your spouse's sexual needs. Have you valued them as much as you value your own? What keeps you from loving your spouse the way he/she likes to be loved? Set up a game plan for overcoming these obstacles.

_____

_____

_____

_____

_____

_____

_____

_____

_____

_____

Day 2
The Daily Special

Let him kiss me with the kisses of his mouth—for your love is more delightful than wine .

—Song of Songs 1:2

Read also the following verses. As you do, note the different ways sexual love is expressed between Solomon and his bride: Song of Songs 1:4; 2:6; 3:1-5; and 4:12–5:1.

Table Talk

It is obvious that God intends sexual love to be expressed in a variety of ways. Sometimes it is fast and intense. Sometimes it is patient and sensitive. It can include kissing, caressing, chasing, holding, intercourse, and so on. Discuss the following questions with your spouse:

1. What are your favorite expressions of sexual love that we share?

2. How often would you like our sexual interaction to be fast and intense? How often would you like it to be slow and sensitive?

3. In what ways do you like to be touched? (Include sexual and non-sexual contact.)

4. What are some of the different ways you feel after our sexual encounters?

Prayer for the Day

Dear God, thank you for the creativity you have included in sexual love. Help me be more creative in loving my spouse. Teach me how to love him/her the way you intended. Make me more patient, more adventurous, more willing, more sensitive, and more in tune with my spouse's needs. I want to be a great lover. Please teach me how. Amen.

Journal Assignment

What do you bring to your lovemaking that enhances the experience for both of you? What does your spouse bring? Brainstorm about some ways you can encourage your spouse in this area without being demanding. What aspects of your lovemaking do you struggle with? Try and figure out if it is because you are resistant to the experience or if it is because it is not good for your relationship. If you are resistant, ask God to work in your heart to make you more willing. If it is unhealthy for your relationship, commit it to prayer and ask God to show you how to talk this through with your spouse without making him/her defensive.

_____

_____

_____

_____

_____

_____

_____

Day 3
The Daily Special

I liken you, my darling, to a mare harnessed to one
of the chariots of Pharaoh. Your cheeks are beautiful
with earrings, your neck with strings of jewels.
—Song of Songs 1:9-10

Consider the compliments in the following verses: Song of Songs 1:16; 4:1-6; 5:10-16; 7:1-9.

Table Talk

One of the most important skills in a sexual relationship is the ability to compliment your spouse. Take inventory of your spouse's abilities and physical attributes and make a list of them. Then sit down with your spouse and read the list out loud, taking time to make as much eye contact as possible.

Prayer for the Day

Dear God, thank you for my husband/wife. Give me eyes to see the best in him/her. Open my eyes to see the beauty in his/her body, personality, and character. Create in me the desire and the discipline to verbally compliment him/her every day. Amen.

Journal Assignment

Write out everything that is attractive about your spouse. Ask God to help you notice some of those things every day. See if you can come up with some phrases to use often that will remind your spouse that he/she holds a special place in your heart. One of the ones I (Bill) use is when Pam comes in the house and says, "It's just me." My response is "No, it's especially you." Commit today to developing a habit of daily letting your spouse know how much he/she is loved.

_____

_____

_____

_____

_____

_____

_____

_____

_____

_____

Day 4
The Daily Special

Beloved: I am a rose of Sharon, a lily of the valleys.
Lover: Like a lily among thorns is my darling among
the maidens.   —Song of Songs 2:1,2

Take note of the way these two lovers build anticipation in their relationship in Song of Songs 2:8-13 and 7:10-12.

Table Talk

A loving, romantic relationship is a dance between two lovers with many twists and turns. In Song of Songs 2:1,2 we see Solomon address the insecurities of his new bride. When she says she is "a rose of Sharon, a lily of the valleys," she is saying she is very ordinary. The rose of Sharon and the lily of the valley grew wild and could be seen anywhere. She is in essence asking Solomon, "Do you think I am just an ordinary woman?"

In Song of Songs 2:8-13 the couple is playing a game building anticipation for their upcoming afternoon together.

In Song of Songs 7:10-12 the couple reminisces about different places they have made love.

Talk with your spouse about these three things. When has your spouse addressed your insecurities with reassurance and caused you to fall even deeper in love? What have you done to build anticipation about time you were able to spend together? What are the places you have enjoyed sexual love together that are your favorites?

Prayer for the Day

Dear God, thank you for romance. Thank you for the variety you have created for lovers to share together. Teach me how to address my spouse's insecurities so we can keep falling in love. Show me how to build anticipation for whatever time I get to spend with my spouse. Give my spouse and me ideas about where we can enjoy one another sexually so we can have a bigger bank of

*memories to share together. Thank you for my spouse
and thank you for the gift of sexual love. Amen.*

Journal Assignment

Think through what you can do to address the insecurities
your spouse seems to struggle with on a regular basis. What can
you say to him/her? What can you do for him/her? How are you
doing at building anticipation for your times together? What can
you do to help your spouse look forward to your next time
alone? List some places you and your spouse can make love
without making you feel uncomfortable. Choose one of these
places and start looking for an opportunity.

_____

_____

_____

_____

_____

_____

_____

_____

_____

_____

_____

Day 5
The Daily Special

Catch for us the foxes, the little foxes that ruin the vineyards, our vineyards that are in bloom.

—Song of Songs 2:15

Read also Song of Songs 5:2-9 to see how this couple faced an awkward sexual encounter.

Table Talk

Every couple experiences times in their sexual relationship that do not go well. Sexual interaction can be frustrating, confusing, and just plain comical. One of the key skills every successful couple develops is the ability to work through these disappointing times. Forgiveness, patience, and a good sense of humor are essential ingredients to any ongoing sexual relationship. Talk through with your spouse times when you handled the awkwardness of your sexual interaction well. What did you appreciate that your spouse did? What are you glad he/she didn't do? What was said that was helpful? What *wasn't* said that was helpful? Thank your spouse verbally for working through the awkwardness.

Prayer for the Day

Dear God, teach me to laugh when love is funny and to cry when love touches my heart at the deepest level. Teach me to forgive when my spouse rejects my advances and to pray for him/her when I reject his/her advances. Renew my love for my spouse over and over again. Make me the kind of lover that my spouse will be glad to be married to. Amen.

Journal Assignment

What are the "little foxes" in your relationship? What are the little things that consistently create frustration and disappointment between the two of you? What can you do to help the "little foxes" become ineffective?

_____

_____

_____

_____

_____

_____

_____

_____

_____

_____

_____

_____

_____

_____

_____

_____

Letter to My Love

Write a letter to your spouse in two parts. In the first part, compliment your spouse's body in as many ways as you can think of. Start at his/her feet and work your way all the way up. End with all the things you like about the face and eyes. Be bold in your descriptions and do not worry about being corny or sounding silly. Your complimentary words about your spouse's body are like treasures of gold given in secret.

In part two, thank your spouse for many of the sexual, romantic times you have spent together. Remembering the past can make for a great future!

Week Six

Waffles and Spaghetti in Conflict

*T*here are five things that women should never, ever ask a guy:

1. "What are you thinking?"

2. "Do you love me?"

3. "Do I look fat?"

4. "Do you think she is prettier than me?"

5. "What would you do if I died?"

What makes these questions so bad is that each one is guaranteed to explode into a major argument and/or divorce if the man does not answer properly, which is to say, dishonestly. For example:

1. "What are you thinking?"

The proper answer to this question, of course, is, "I'm sorry if I've been pensive, dear. I was just reflecting on what a warm, wonderful, caring, thoughtful, intelligent, beautiful woman you are, and what a lucky guy I am to have met you." Obviously, this statement bears no resemblance whatsoever to what the guy was really thinking at the time, which was most likely one of five things: Baseball; Football; How fat you are; How much prettier she is than you; or How he would spend the insurance money if you died.

The other questions also have only one right answer but many wrong answers.

2. "Do you love me?"

The correct answer to this question is, "Yes." For those guys who feel the need to be more elaborate, you may answer, "Yes, dear." Wrong answers include: I suppose so; Would it make you feel better if I said yes?; That depends on what you mean by "love"; Does it matter?; or Who, me?

3. "Do I look fat?"

The correct male response to this question is to quickly, confidently, and emphatically state, "No, of course not," and then quickly leave the room. Wrong answers include: I wouldn't call you fat, but I wouldn't call you thin either; Compared to what? A little extra weight looks good on you; I've seen fatter; or Could you repeat the question? I was thinking about your insurance policy.

4. "Do you think she's prettier than me?"

The "she" in the question could be an ex-girlfriend, a passerby you were staring at so hard that you almost caused a traffic accident, or an actress in a movie you just saw. In any case, the correct response is, "No, you are much prettier." Wrong answers include: Not prettier, just pretty in a different way; I don't know how one goes about rating such things; Yes, but I bet you have a better personality; Only in the sense that she's younger and thinner; or Could you repeat the question? I was thinking about your insurance policy.

5. "What would you do if I died?"

Correct answer: "Dearest love, in the event of your untimely demise, life would cease to have meaning for me, and I would be forced to hurl myself under the front tires of the first Domino's Pizza truck that came my way." This might be the most awkward question of the lot, as is illustrated by the following exchange:

"Dear," said the wife, "what would you do if I died?"

"Why, dear, I would be extremely upset," said the husband. "Why do you ask such a question?"

"Would you remarry?" persevered the wife.

"No, of course not, dear," said the husband.

"Don't you like being married?" asked the wife.

"Of course I do, dear," he said.

"Then why wouldn't you remarry?"

"All right," said the husband, "I'd remarry."

"You would?" asked the wife, looking vaguely hurt.

"Yes," said the husband.

"Would you sleep with her in our bed?" asked the wife after a long pause.

"Well, yes, I suppose I would," replied the husband.

"I see," said the wife indignantly. "And would you let her wear my old clothes?"

"I suppose, if she wanted to," said the husband.

"Really," said the wife icily. "And would you take down the pictures of me and replace them with pictures of her?"

"Yes. I think that would be the correct thing to do."

"Is that so?" said the wife, leaping to her feet. "And I suppose you'd let her play with my golf clubs, too!"

"Of course not, dear," said the husband. "She's left-handed..."[1]

Slips of the tongue can get both men and women into all kinds of trouble! Let's look this week at how we handle those moments when we disagree with one another.

Day 1
The Daily Special

A man finds joy in giving an apt reply—and how good is a timely word!   —Proverbs 15:23

For more good advice on conflict management, read the following verses; Proverbs 12:18; 15:28; 16:23; and 25:11.

Table Talk

One of the ways to head off unnecessary conflict in your marriage is to "cut the hot lead" in discussions. What are phrases and/or reactions in your relationship that tend to create tension? How have you been successful in the past in heading off the tension? What new ways would you like to try in the future to see if you can lower the conflict level in your relationship?

Prayer for the Day

Lord, give me the right words to say at the right time to head off unnecessary conflict with my spouse. Help me to see problems coming before they happen and give me the strength to not add to the turmoil. Amen.

Journal Assignment

Make a list of the unnecessary conflicts you have had with your spouse during the past few months. Do you see any patterns in the turmoil? Can you identify the underlying causes of the tension? Write out a strategy of how you can talk with your spouse about these underlying reasons.

_____

_____

_____

_____

_____

_____

_____

_____

_____

_____

_____

_____

_____

_____

_____

_____

_____

Day 2
The Daily Special

The wise in heart are called discerning, and pleasant
words promote instruction.   —Proverbs 16:21

Read also what Proverbs 18:21 and 25:15 have to say about
the power of words.

Table Talk

Talk about how good are you as a couple with
saying, "This hurt my feelings," and having it *help*
your conversation. If you are successful in doing
this, what do you think is the source of your success? If you are not successful in doing this, what
do you think is the obstacle to your success? Then
talk about how you would like your spouse to
respond when you say something like, "This hurt
my feelings."

Prayer for the Day

*Lord, I want my spouse to feel it is safe to talk with
me. When he/she sounds the alert to hurt feelings,
help me be responsive. Give me a sensitive heart to have
compassion and a willing tongue to stop the hurt.
Amen.*

Journal Assignment

All of us say things that hurt the ones we love. What are the
most common things you say that hurt your spouse? Why do

you think you say them? What need is met in your life when you say hurtful things to your spouse? Can you think of another way to get this need met that would be healthier for your relationship?

_____

_____

_____

_____

_____

_____

_____

_____

_____

Day 3
The Daily Special

Leave your simple ways and you will live; walk in the way of understanding. —Proverbs 9:6

Read also Proverbs 1:5 and 2:6 for insight into wisdom and understanding.

Table Talk

Most often, the things that irritate you about your spouse are the same things you love about your spouse. If your spouse is sensitive, you will feel as though you are sharing him/her with too many other people. If your spouse is decisive, you will feel pressure from the seemingly demanding tone of that same decisiveness. Discuss with each other the characteristics you love about one another and the irritations those same characteristics bring to your relationship. How can you use your irritations to remind you of what you love about the one you married?

Prayer for the Day

Dear Jesus, it is so strange that the things I love about my mate are the same things that sometimes drive me crazy. Give me the grace to see the things I love in the irritations I feel toward my spouse. Remind me today that my spouse can also be irritated by what he/she loves about me, and increase my ability to be patient with him/her. Amen.

Journal Assignment

Make a list of the characteristics you most appreciate about your spouse. Across from each characteristic, write down how it could be an irritation to you. Then write out a plan of how you can focus on the things you love when they present themselves as irritations.

_____

_____

_____

_____

_____

_____

_____

_____

_____

_____

Day 4
The Daily Special

Likewise the tongue is a small part of the body, but it makes great boasts. Consider what a great forest is set on fire by a small spark. The tongue also is a fire, a world of evil among the parts of the body. It corrupts the whole person, sets the whole course of his life on fire, and is itself set on fire by hell.

—James 3:5-6

Read Proverbs 12:14 and 16:23 and consider a little further the importance of words.

Table Talk

Words are very powerful. They can build up or they can tear down. Because of this, couples often find themselves in conflict but do not understand why. Their differences have collided and an argument has ensued. If you, as a couple, don't know what started the argument, you won't know how to finish it. If you haven't read pages 115-118 in *Men Are Like Waffles—Women Are Like Spaghetti* about passwords, do it now. Then discuss as a couple what your passwords are. If you don't have any yet, brainstorm together what might work for you.

Prayer for the Day

Lord, give me wisdom to know when we are having arguments simply because we are different. Give us passwords that will recapture these conversations and build into our relationship rather than tear it down. When our passwords are used, help me be responsive quickly to them. Amen.

Journal Assignment

What areas of your life continually irritate your spouse? Write them down and ask these questions about each of them:

1. Is this an area of my life that should change?

2. If so, what is my plan to make the change?

3. Is this an area that shouldn't change in my life and should be committed to prayer on behalf of my spouse?

_____

_____

_____

_____

_____

_____

_____

_____

_____

_____

_____

_____

Day 5
The Daily Special

Bear with each other and forgive whatever griev-
ances you may have against one another. Forgive as
the Lord forgave you. —Colossians 3:13

The amazing grace of forgiveness is beautifully illustrated
between Joseph and his brothers. Read Genesis 50:15-21 and let
these verses touch your heart.

Table Talk

Sometimes the only thing that will calm a conflict is
forgiveness. How has forgiveness affected your relationship? How has the forgiveness you have received
through the gospel of Jesus Christ impacted the way
your relationship operates? Thank one another for
the times you have been forgiven and talk about how
you can make sure that forgiveness remains an active
part of your relationship.

Prayer for the Day

Lord, I need to be a good forgiver. Thank you for dying for me and forgiving me for all the things I have done. Help me to forgive my spouse the way you forgive me. Make me good at forgiving the daily disappointments and help me to keep very short accounts with my mate. Amen.

Journal Assignment

Write a letter to yourself explaining all the reasons why you should forgive everyone for anything that is done to hurt you. Be sure to think about the following: bitterness has an insatiable appetite and will not stop until it has affected your entire life, you become like the people you don't forgive because you focus too intensely on them, and anyone you do not forgive has emotional control in your life. At the end of the letter, give yourself permission to forgive everyone!

_____

_____

_____

_____

_____

_____

_____

_____

_____

Letter to My L♥ve

Write a letter of commitment to your spouse. In the letter include the following: a dedication to finish every argument, a commitment to use your conflicts to rediscover the things you love about one another, a vow to develop and use passwords to avoid unnecessary arguments, and a covenant to forgive actively.

Week Seven

Waffles and Spaghetti Achieving Together

*H*ere is a story about a couple who learned about the blessings of doing work together:

> When we arrived at our Washington, D.C., hotel for a business convention, the massive lobby was buzzing with clusters of talkative women. We soon learned that we were sharing the hotel with another convention, the Romance Writers of America.
>
> There were very few men among the hundreds of women romance writers, but during the week I spotted one gentleman sporting a distinctive T-shirt.
>
> On the front it read: "My wife writes romance novels." On the back it said: "And I do the research."[1]

Cooperating together for success can be fun and good for your relationship! This week's focus is on how you complement one another in ways that allow your gifts and talents to multiply.

Day 1
The Daily Special

Again, it will be like a man going on a journey, who called his servants and entrusted his property to them. To one he gave five talents of money, to another two talents, and to another one talent, each according to his ability. Then he went on his journey. The man who had received the five talents went at once and put his money to work and gained five more. So also, the one with the two talents gained two more. But the man who had received the one talent went off, dug a hole in the ground and hid his master's money.

After a long time the master of those servants returned and settled accounts with them. The man who had received the five talents brought the other five. "Master," he said, "you entrusted me with five talents. See, I have gained five more."

His master replied, "Well done, good and faithful servant! You have been faithful with a few things; I will put you in charge of many things. Come and share your master's happiness!" —Matthew 25:14-20

Table Talk

Compliment your spouse. What do you see are his or her most precious talents?

Prayer for the Day

Lord, help me support my spouse as he/she gives her talents to you. Amen.

Journal Assignment

How can you be a better support to your mate as he/she seeks to maximize the use of his/her talent? Place yourself in his/her shoes. What would help you more?

_____

_____

_____

_____

_____

_____

_____

_____

_____

_____

_____

_____

_____

_____

_____

_____

_____

_____

_____

Day 2
The Daily Special

The man with the two talents also came. "Master," he said, "you entrusted me with two talents; see, I have gained two more."

His master replied, "Well done, good and faithful servant! You have been faithful with a few things; I will put you in charge of many things. Come and share your master's happiness!"

Then the man who had received the one talent came. "Master," he said, "I knew that you are a hard man, harvesting where you have not sown and gathering where you have not scattered seed. So I was afraid and went out and hid your talent in the ground. See, here is what belongs to you."

His master replied, "You wicked, lazy servant! So you knew that I harvest where I have not sown and gather where I have not scattered seed? Well then, you should have put my money on deposit with the bankers, so that when I returned I would have received it back with interest.

"Take the talent from him and give it to the one who has the ten talents. For everyone who has will be given more, and he will have an abundance. Whoever does not have, even what he has will be taken from him."

—Matthew 25:22-29

Table Talk

Each of you answer the following questions:

1. How talented do you think God has made us as a couple? Are we a five-talent couple, a two-talent couple, or a one-talent couple?

2. What do you think are our greatest talents as a couple?

3. Are we maximizing each of our talents for the greatest glory for God?

4. Are we hiding any of our talents out of fear?

Prayer for the Day

Lord, give us courage so we might serve you, work to our potential, and maximize the talent you entrusted to each of us, to us as a couple, and to our family. Amen.

Journal Assignment

What brings out fear in you? When a new opportunity arises, how do you respond? How does your mate respond? Is your fear holding you or your mate back from achieving your potential at work, at home, or in relationships?

_____

_____

_____

_____

_____

_____

_____

_____

Day 3
The Daily Special

As Jesus and his disciples were on their way, he came to a village where a woman named Martha opened her home to him. She had a sister called Mary, who sat at the Lord's feet listening to what he said. But Martha was distracted by all the preparations that had to be made. She came to him and asked, "Lord, don't you care that my sister has left me to do the work by myself? Tell her to help me!"

"Martha, Martha," the Lord answered, "you are worried and upset about many things, but only one thing is needed. Mary has chosen what is better, and it will not be taken away from her."   —Luke 10:38-42

Table Talk

Each of you answer, "Am I choosing 'the better part'? What care of the world, concern over achievement, or constant career pressure threatens to pull me or has pulled me from my higher priorities?"

Prayer for the Day

Lord, help us keep first things first. Amen.

Journal Assignment

Sit at Jesus' feet today. Pray, "Lord, show me any way that I might be shortcutting my relationship with you and what you want me to do about it." Write out the thoughts that come to your mind after you pray.

_____

_____

_____

_____

_____

_____

_____

_____

_____

_____

_____

_____

_____

_____

Day 4
The Daily Special

"My food," said Jesus, "is to do the will of him who sent me and to finish his work."   —John 4:34

Table Talk

Discuss your goals in your career with your spouse. What do you most enjoy doing when it comes to work? What do you think is God's will for your career? What do you hope to accomplish in the next ten years? How do your career goals fit in with your family life?

Prayer for the Day

Lord, help us consider the impact of our choices on those we love most. Amen.

Journal Assignment

Are you comfortable with the way you make decisions? Do you ask before a decision, "What do you think, God?" Do you have a "seeking the will of God" attitude? Do you ask your spouse his or her opinion? Write out a strategy of how you can develop, or further develop, a "seeking the will of God" attitude.

_____

_____

_____

_____

_____

_____

_____

_____

Day 5
The Daily Special

For even when we were with you, we gave you this
rule: "If a man will not work, he shall not eat."
—2 Thessalonians 3:10

Table Talk

Discuss these two questions as a couple: Are we
desiring enough financial achievement so that we are
not a burden to others, the church, our family, or the
government? What are we doing to help develop a
healthy work ethic in ourselves, in our kids, and in
others we have an impact on? Today's verse says those
who do not work should not be helped with food.
How do you decide whom to be generous with and
whom to withhold help from?

Prayer for the Day

*Lord, help us be responsible in all areas, especially to
one another and to our children. Amen.*

Journal Assignment

What are some financial goals that would help you be a good
steward and godly provider for your mate and family? What do
you think God wants you to tackle first? How do you think your
spouse would answer this question?

_____

_____

_____

_____

_____

_____

_____

_____

_____

_____

_____

_____

_____

_____

_____

_____

_____

_____

_____

_____

_____

_____

_____

_____

_____

Letter to My Love

Write your spouse a letter of support. Think through what you appreciate most about his/her talents, use of money, or commitment to help provide. Choose the words you think would best motivate your spouse to realize his/her goals in life.

Week Eight
Waffles and Spaghetti at Home

There's nothing like everyday responsibilities to demonstrate how men and women view life at home. Take children and laundry, for example:

◈ A woman knows all about her children. She knows about dentist appointments and soccer games and romances and best friends and favorite foods and secret fears and hopes and dreams.

◈ A man is vaguely aware of some short people living in the house.

◈ A woman will do laundry every couple of days.

◈ A man will wear every article of clothing he owns, including his surgical pants that were hip about eight years ago, before he will do his laundry. When he is finally out of clothes, he will wear a dirty sweatshirt inside out, rent a U-Haul to take his mountain of clothes to the Laundromat, and expect to meet a beautiful woman while he is there.[1]

We all bring preconceptions into marriage. You probably brought some opinions on who should vacuum, dust, rake, or change the light bulbs. Many arguments could be avoided if we'd just talk out expectations, and keep talking until we both get on the same page. This week's exercises should help you do just that!

Day 1
The Daily Special

Submit to one another out of reverence for Christ.
—Ephesians 5:21

Table Talk

The word "submit" is a military term, meaning a voluntary choice to rank yourself under another. How does having an attitude of *mutual* submission create a home environment that brings a spirit of unity and cooperation? Why would having an attitude of voluntarily choosing to rank yourself under your mate in an area show an attitude of respect? Give your mate a compliment. In what area around the home do you feel your mate gives you the greatest sense of respect or cooperation?

Prayer for the Day

Lord, give me an attitude of respect and cooperation. Help me see the bigger picture and help us find a workable system for life around our home. Amen.

Journal Assignment

How do you feel when your spouse asks you to do something around the house? Are you offended? Are you willing? Are you cooperative? Do you procrastinate or give excuses? When your mate is obviously struggling with a responsibility, do you jump to help or do you have an attitude?

_____

_____

_____

_____

_____

_____

_____

_____

_____

Day 2
The Daily Special

Each one of you also must love his wife as he loves himself, and the wife must respect her husband.
—Ephesians 5:31

Read this verse in the context of Ephesians 5:22-31 to help you understand God's view of the relationship between a husband and wife.

Table Talk

Now we're entering controversial territory. What do you think is a wife's role? What is a husband's role? Let's look at the text. A wife is to:

❖ Submit to her husband as unto the Lord.

❖ Submit because her husband is the head of her in the same way Jesus is the head of the church.

❖ Submit in everything.

❖ A wife must respect her husband.

Reread the story of our move to San Diego in *Men Are Like Waffles—Women Are Like Spaghetti*, pages 137-140.

To show respect to Bill, I had to:

1. See Bill as God sees Bill—a man worthy of honor because God created him.

2. Talk to Bill the way God talks to Bill—with loving, encouraging but honest words.

3. Treat Bill the way God treats Bill—by building him up with kindness.

Husbands, which one of these three things does your wife seem to be best at or do most naturally?

Now for the husbands. The text says a husband is to:

❖ Love his wife as Christ loved the church (Jesus died for the church!).

❖ Cleanse her by the washing of the Word (this means a husband is to encourage his wife to develop a life of growth and maturity so that she can become all God intended her to be).

❖ Love her as his own body . . . "he feeds and cares for it." (Feed and care is the picture of nourish and cherish. Much like a mother bird goes out in search of food for the young chicks, so a husband is to search out the best ways to nourish and cherish his wife so she can rise to her God-given potential.)

Wives, which of these three does your husband seem to most enjoy or do naturally or with ease? Thank him.

Prayer for the Day

Wives: Lord, help me respect and submit to my husband as unto you. Lord, I want to trust your will to be accomplished through my husband's love for me. Amen.

Husbands: Lord, help me love my wife as you loved the church, laying down my life and my desires. And help me go in search of those things that will help my wife become all that you designed her to be. Amen.

Journal Assignment

Okay, now let's look at what is the most difficult for you in the area of husband/wife relations. Look at the lists again. Which area is it most unnatural or most difficult for you to carry out the commands of Scripture in this text? Why do you think it is so hard? What obstacle in your heart or mind do you think you need to overcome in order to fulfill this text and obey God? Remember, you can't change your spouse, but you can change your attitude and you can pray that God will change you!

_____

_____

_____

_____

_____

_____

_____

_____

_____

_____

Day 3
The Daily Special

Wives, submit to your husbands, as is fitting in the Lord. Husbands, love your wives and do not be harsh with them.

—Colossians 3:18-19

Read also 1 Timothy 3:11 for important character traits that every married person needs.

Table Talk

Husbands: Which of the traits in the verses above would a stranger, just meeting your wife, quickly see in her? (Is she worthy of respect? Are her words gracious? Is her behavior temperate (not extreme)? Is she trustworthy?)

Wives: Give your husband your favorite example of a time he was gentle with you, instead of being harsh.

Prayer for the Day

Men: Lord, please help me control my temper. Let me not say or do anything that would be seen by my wife as harsh. Amen.

Women: Lord, help me live a life worthy of respect and trust by my words and my actions. Amen.

Journal Assignment

Again, take a hard look in the mirror. Guys, when are you most apt to be harsh, and what is your plan to correct your harsh behavior? Ladies, are you living a life so that your husband can respect and trust you? What changes might you need to make?

_____

_____

_____

_____

_____

_____

_____

_____

_____

_____

_____

Day 4
The Daily Special

Wives, in the same way be submissive to your husbands so that, if any of them do not believe the word, they may be won over without words by the behavior of their wives…Husbands, in the same way be considerate as you live with your wives, and treat them with respect as the weaker partner and as heirs with you of the gracious gift of life, so that nothing will hinder your prayers.

—1 Peter 3:1,7

Table Talk

Now we see some of the benefits of living the way God wants you to live with your spouse. First Peter explains that when a wife chooses to submit to her husband (rather than nag, argue, give the silent treatment, or explode), then he may be won over without a word. The context of this passage is speaking to women whose husbands are not walking with the Lord; however, there are many times believing wives *think* their husbands who are believers are not listening to God! So some of the same dynamics can take place in these kinds of relationships too.

The text in 1 Peter for the men explains that when they are considerate and respect their mates as a gracious gift, their prayers aren't hindered. It seems as though God isn't very interested in listening and answering the prayers of an inconsiderate, disrespectful man.

So the questions for today are then:

◈ Wives, what was the most recent example of a considerate act your husband did for you?

◈ Husbands, when recently did your wife give you the gift of going along with your wishes without a fight?

Prayer for the Day

Lord, help us be considerate of one another today. Help our actions toward one another be a gift to you today. Amen.

Journal Assignment

Ladies, as a woman who is a director of women's ministries, a pastor's wife, and a women's speaker, I can say that our number one problem in relationships is that we are control freaks. We feel we have *the* plan, we feel we should always have the last word, and we feel life would be better if our husbands and kids would just get in line! But there is only one God, and we're not it! Write out a commitment to God that you will rank your "say" under God's today. As an experiment for one day (you choose the day this week) try allowing your husband to truly lead. Say "Yes, dear" a few more times. Go with his opinion without a big argument. Just try it! See if you can go one day fully trusting your husband's leadership!

Men, write out a commitment to God to value your wife, value her opinion, and value her contribution to the family. In our ministry, we daily see men causing their marriages to decay out of neglect. They seem to have just opted out of life and responsibility. Some make rude comments or become rude in their behaviors. Others seem to just check out. Write out ways you will be more considerate of your mate (try to notice if you have stopped doing the little things that show big consideration: carry the groceries in, pack the car, put gas in the car for her, fix something around the house, and so on.) Choose a day this week to be your wife's personal assistant (but don't tell her—just do it!)

_____

_____

_____

_____

_____

_____

_____

_____

_____

_____

_____

_____

Day 5
The Daily Special

There is neither Jew nor Greek, slave nor free, male nor female, for you are all one in Christ Jesus.
—Galatians 3:28

Table Talk

Do gender stereotypes factor into your decisions regarding who does what around the house? Read pages 152-158 of *Men Are Like Waffles—Women Are Like Spaghetti*. If you haven't completed the exercise on pages 154-155, make a date and do it. Then write out who is best at what and who feels the most emotion about certain jobs. Delegate according to gifts, talents, and passion rather than stereotypes. To start the conversation rolling, share the answer to this question: Who was responsible for what around the house when you were growing up? For example, in the home I (Pam) grew up in, my dad's domain was the garage, barn, and yard, and Mom's was anything and everything in the house. However, just down the street, there was a family where the dad loved to cook and the mom was seen mowing each week. What unspoken, unwritten expectations are you bringing into your marriage from your childhood years?

Prayer for the Day

Lord, free us to see who has been gifted by you to do what around our home. Let us follow your leading, not traditions or outside expectations. Amen.

Journal Assignment

Of the household chores that need to be done, which ones do you enjoy doing the most? Which ones do you dislike doing? Which ones are you willing to do even though you neither like nor dislike them? Write out a strategy of how you can approach your spouse with a plan for dividing responsibilities in a way that is most advantageous for both of you.

_____

_____

_____

_____

_____

_____

_____

_____

_____

_____

_____

_____

_____

_____

_____

_____

_____

Letter to My Love

Write a letter to your mate that communicates the respect and admiration you have for him/her and the way he/she makes your house a home. Are there commitments and changes that you have made before Christ as a result of this lesson that you want to communicate to your mate?

Week Nine

Waffles and Spaghetti As Parents

Let's look at some children's views of love and marriage:

Concerning the Proper Age to Get Married.
Once I'm done with kindergarten, I'm going to find
me a wife.
—Bert, age 5

How Did Your Mom and Dad Meet?
They were at a dance party at a friend's house. Then
they went for a drive, but their car broke down. It was
a good thing, because it gave them a chance to find
out about their values.
—Lottie, age 9

When Is It Okay to Kiss Someone?
You should never kiss a girl unless you have enough
bucks to buy her a ring and her own VCR, 'cause
she'll want to have videos of the wedding.
—Allan, age 10[1]

These kid quips make us smile, but sometimes as we seek to parent, those same cute kids can cause us to disagree, and that can create an atmosphere contrary to romance. This week, see how parenting can bring you closer rather than push you apart.

Day 1
The Daily Special

We were gentle among you, like a mother caring for her little children. We loved you so much that we were delighted to share with you not only the gospel of God but our lives as well, because you had become so dear to us... For you know that we dealt with each of you as a father deals with his own children, encouraging, comforting and urging you to live lives worthy of God, who calls you into his kingdom and glory.
—1 Thessalonians 2:7,8,11,12

Table Talk

When the apostle Paul wanted to use an illustration about the kind of deep care extended to those in Thessalonica, he went to the most primary relationships of love—a mother and a father. Mom (some translate this nursing mother) tenderly cared for children imparting her very life. Dad encouraged, comforted, and urged his offspring to live a life worthy for God. And what were the results in Paul's ministry? The Thessalonians accepted the Word of God. We can anticipate similar results if we have similar behaviors toward our own children.

Dad: Compliment Mom today on how she tenderly cares for the children or on how she has sacrificed (given her life) for the kids.

Mom: Compliment Dad today on how he encourages the kids or the way he comforts them or the way he leads them into a stronger relationship with God.

Prayer for the Day

Lord, we lift ourselves up to you today as parents (or future parents). Develop in us the traits Paul talked about—tenderness, sacrifice, comfort, encouragement, and leadership. Amen.

Journal Assignment

To become a better parent, become a better person! Look again at Paul's descriptions. Are any of those roles more difficult for you? (Do you have a hard time encouraging, giving comfort, or sacrificing? Are you uncomfortable with the role of giving spiritual leadership?) Look around. Do you know other parents who are comfortable in the area you feel deficient? Watch how they relate to their children this week and make notes below on what you learn from them.[2]

_____

_____

_____

_____

_____

_____

Day 2
The Daily Special

When I was a boy in my father's house, still tender, and an only child of my mother, he taught me and said, "Lay hold of my words with all your heart; keep my commands and you will live."   —Proverbs 4:3,4

Read also Proverbs 4:5–5:2.

Table Talk

What do you learn from the verses above about the father from the son's description in this section from Proverbs? What is one behavior of the Proverbs parent you'd like to emulate today to one or more of your children? Each of you share one trait or choice and how you can implement it into your parenting this week.

Prayer for the Day

Lord, help us pass on to our children the truths they need to know about you and about life. Amen.

Journal Assignment

It is good advice to tune our ears to God's wisdom. Read the passage above again. What are the results or benefits from living a life where you seek godly wisdom? (Underline the results.)

Where can you go, whom can you talk to, and what kinds of organizations and resources will give these kinds of godly insights? Make a list of five resources (books, magazines, conferences, websites, small groups, etc.). See how many resources you can integrate into your life to gain more parenting wisdom.

_____

_____

_____

_____

_____

_____

_____

Day 3
The Daily Special

Train a child in the way he should go, and when he is old he will not turn from it.
                                                        —Proverbs 22:6

Table Talk

It goes without saying that it is important to keep gender differences in mind as you "train up a child." Boys and girls react to life in completely different ways. What information from chapter 9 in *Men Are Like Waffles—Women Are Like Spaghetti* helped you better understand your son/daughter? (If you haven't read this chapter, read it as soon as you can.) What parenting changes might you want to adapt or change as you integrate this new information?

Prayer for the Day

Lord, help me appreciate the children I meet that are the opposite gender from me. Give me insight and guidance as I deal with my own "pasta princess" or "Belgian boy." Amen.

Journal Assignment

Dad, list all the things girls love. Mom, list all the things boys love. Write out a commitment to God where you name one thing the child of the opposite gender loves that you are willing to learn to love.

_____

_____

_____

_____

_____

_____

_____

_____

_____

_____

_____

_____

_____

Day 4
The Daily Special

Fathers, do not exasperate your children; instead, bring them up in the training and instruction of the Lord.

—Ephesians 6:4

Fathers, do not embitter your children, or they will become discouraged.

—Colossians 3:21

Table Talk

According to God's Word, what mistakes can men make to cause their children to be exasperated or embittered toward their fathers, toward their parents, toward authorities of all kinds, or toward God?

Prayer for the Day

Dad pray: Lord, help me not embitter or exasperate my children. God, I need your wisdom, guidance and strength. Amen.

Mom pray: Lord, help me support my husband in a way that will enable him to succeed as a dad. Help my husband to have clear insight into each of our kids so he can have a powerful and positive impact on their lives. Amen.

Journal Assignment

Think of your own father. What do you think he did that was an example you'd like to follow? What mistakes do you feel he made that you want to avoid?

_____

_____

_____

_____

_____

_____

_____

_____

Day 5
The Daily Special

Charm is deceptive, and beauty is fleeting; but a woman who fears the Lord is to be praised. Give her the reward she has earned, and let her works bring her praise at the city gate.   —Proverbs 31:30,31

Read Proverbs 31:10-31 and take note of all the action words.

Table Talk
In the above verses from Proverbs 31, underline all the verbs. Each of you talk about what traits (shown by the action words) each of your own mothers possessed. Which ones do you each see as most vital so that your children would want to rise up and bless their mother saying, "I had a great mom!"

Prayer for the Day

Mom pray: Lord, layer the most important traits into my life. Keep me from thinking I have to be perfect, and also keep me dependent on you. Amen.

Dad pray: Lord, teach me how to best encourage my wife so she will be a great mom. Help my wife develop in her life the traits that will best influence our kids. Amen.

Journal Assignment

Moms, Proverbs 31 was a tribute written by a son, a composite poem, that gave praise to his mother's accomplishments over the course of her WHOLE life. Which verbs from the passage are you doing now and feel God wants you to continue with, and which are verbs (actions) for a later season in your life?

Dads, look how busy the Proverbs 31 woman was. Of the traits above, are there any you could take on to lighten your wife's load? Delegate any to the children? Pay someone else to do it so she can focus during this season in life on her top priorities?

_____

_____

_____

_____

_____

_____

_____

Letter to My Love

Write a thank-you note to your spouse complimenting his/her parenting.

Week Ten

*Waffles and Spaghetti Meeting
Each Other's Key Needs*

An elderly couple came back from a wedding one afternoon and were in a pretty romantic mood. While sitting on their love seat, the elderly woman looked at her companion and said, "I remember when you used to kiss me every chance you had." The old man, feeling a bit obliged, leaned over and gave her a peck on the cheek. Then she said, "I also remember when you used to hold my hand at every opportunity." The old man, again feeling obligated, reached over and gently placed his hand on hers. The elderly woman then stated, "I also remember when you used to nibble on my neck and send chills down my spine." This time the old man had a blank stare on his face and started to get up off the couch. As he began to walk out of the living room his wife asked, "Was it something I said? Where are you going?" The old man looked at her and replied, "I'm going in the other room to get my teeth!"[1]

How can you have a love that will last a lifetime? See your spouse from God's point of view, and seek to learn the inner workings of his/her soul. This week we'll discover what really makes us tick.

Day 1
The Daily Special

It is better to take refuge in the LORD than to trust in man. It is better to take refuge in the LORD than to trust in princes.

—Psalm 118:8-9

Table Talk

When you fell in love, you might have thought, "Oh, she is like a princess, a dream come true," or "He is so regal, such a glorious man!" It is easy to place all your trust in another person when you are in love. God made love to meet needs, but no human love, not even in marriage, can meet *all* our needs. In Psalm 118 the psalmist says, "It is better to take refuge in the LORD than to trust in man." Think about places of refuge: under a spreading tree in a rainstorm, in a cool cave on a hot summer's day, behind a locked door in an unsafe neighborhood.

Think about your life right now. What circumstance is most threatening or feels unsafe to you? Explain one way you need God to be your refuge because your mate *can't* help. For example, if things are bad at work, your mate can't shelter you from your boss's harsh words or get you a new job.

Prayer for the Day

Lord, you are our refuge and strength, our very present help in time of need. Please shelter us today. Amen.

Journal Assignment

In what area have you expected your mate to meet a need only God can meet? Are you looking to your mate for your life's purpose? Are you expecting your mate to make you feel a certain way?

_____

_____

_____

_____

_____

_____

_____

_____

_____

_____

_____

_____

_____

Day 2
The Daily Special

Some trust in chariots and some in horses, but we trust in the name of the Lord our God. —Psalm 20:7

Read also about what the following verses have to say about security and success in life: Psalm 44:6 and 49:12-15.

Table Talk

Today's verses explain some things not to trust in—counterfeits that will disappoint:

- ❖ Chariots and horses: tools for battle, signs of wealth
- ❖ Bows: personal weapons of warfare
- ❖ Yourself: even you are fallible!

In your relationship with your spouse, are you trusting in one of these things to meet a need:

- ❖ Signs of wealth: Are you throwing money at a problem, issue, or unmet need in hopes that it will go away?
- ❖ Weapons of personal battle: Are you throwing out words, accusations, or other weapons of personal attack to defend yourself?
- ❖ Yourself: Have you got the martyr attitude going? (You might find yourself saying things like, "Fine, I'll just handle it!" or "All right, I'll just do it myself!")

Which counterfeit do you find yourself picking up when things are rough in your relationship?

Prayer for the Day

Lord, please be my defense and shield. I don't want to trust in counterfeits to meet my needs; I choose to trust only in you. Amen.

Journal Assignment

Think of a time you trusted in a counterfeit to fill a need. What was the result?

For example, when Bill is busy or if I feel he isn't understanding where I am coming from on an issue, it's easy for me to pull out my martyr attitude of "Okay, fine. I'll just handle it myself!" The result is that Bill might end up feeling rejected, left out, or hurt. So now I don't just have one problem (my unmet need), I have another new problem I helped create!

In your situation, what would you do differently next time?

_____

_____

_____

_____

_____

_____

_____

_____

_____

Day 3
The Daily Special

Trust in the LORD and do good; dwell in the land and enjoy safe pasture. Delight yourself in the LORD and he will give you the desires of your heart. Commit your way to the LORD; trust in him and he will do this: He will make your righteousness shine like the dawn, the justice of your cause like the noonday sun.

—Psalm 37:3-6

Table Talk

These verses have been favorites of ours since our dating days because they outline what trusting in God looks like!

If you trust in God you will :

❧ Do good.

❧ Dwell in the land (hang out where God is: that is, attend church, read your Bible, listen to Christian radio/TV, read Christian books, spend time with people who know God, etc.).

❧ Delight yourself in him (cultivate an attitude of gratitude, praise him, sing to him, obey him).

❧ Commit your way to him (learn to say and pray, "God, what do you think about this? How shall I proceed?").

The results:

❧ You will enjoy safe pasture (your emotions will be protected).

❧ He'll do it (you'll get your desires. Because you've asked, "What do you think, God?" you will begin praying more in line with God's heart for you, and that means more and more of your desires will be fulfilled because they are actually God's desires for you).

◈ Make your righteousness shine (trust means you don't have to defend yourself. God will make your character shine, and the truth will come out and reign in your relationships eventually if you keep trusting).

Which of these characteristics and results of trusting God is most meaningful to you? How can you integrate these characteristics into your relationship?

Prayer for the Day

Lord, help us place our trust in you today. Help us commit our plans, our wishes, and our dreams into your care and ask, "What do you think, God? Where shall we go from here?" Amen.

Journal Assignment

Reread the steps of trust. Which is hardest for you and why? Write a prayer asking God to help out in that area.

_____

_____

_____

_____

_____

_____

Day 4
The Daily Special

Those who know your name will trust in you, for you,
LORD, have never forsaken those who seek you.

—Psalm 9:10

Read also Psalm 52:8 and 125:1.

Table Talk

What are some of the results of trusting in God
according to the verses above? Which result would
you like to experience currently?

Prayer for the Day

*Lord, help me by faith to step out and daily trust that
you will never forsake me. Amen.*

Journal Assignment

There may be areas in your relationship in which you feel
forsaken or forgotten by your mate or by the Lord. Name the
area and commit its care to the hands of a loving God. You might
choose to write one of these verses in your own words and make
it your prayer: Psalm 56:3,4; 62:8; or 143:8.

_____

_____

_____

_____

_____

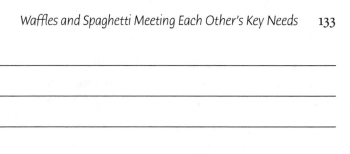

Day 5
The Daily Special

I will say of the LORD, "He is my refuge and my fortress, my God, in whom I trust."   —Psalm 91:2

Read also Proverbs 3:5-6.

Table Talk

What changes have you seen in your relationship as a result of this study? Where have you quit trusting in your ways and started doing things God's ways? Name at least one positive change you have applied to your marriage.

Prayer for the Day

Lord, help us to always think of you as a refuge and a fortress. Trusting in you will help us have the relationship we have always desired. Help us use our differences for us in our marriage. Amen.

Journal Assignment

What in this last chapter hit closest to home? How can you better allow God to meet your need for either security or simplicity?

_____

_____

_____

_____

_____

_____

_____

_____

_____

_____

_____

_____

_____

_____

_____

_____

_____

_____

Letter to My Love

Write a letter thanking your spouse for taking the time and making the effort to do this study with you. Make special note of the ways he/she has sought to make your relationship stronger, better, closer. Praise your mate for loving you enough to invest together in the growth of your marriage.

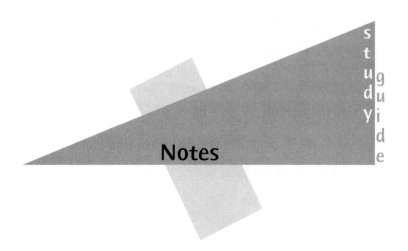

study guide

Notes

Week One — *The Preparation of Waffles and Spaghetti*

1. www.marthabolton.com. For more marriage humor, Martha Bolton, *I Love You…Still* (Grand Rapids, MI: Fleming H. Revell, 2000).

Week Two —*Waffles and Spaghetti Communicating*

1. <www.hitched.co.uk>

Week Three — *Waffles and Spaghetti Relaxing*

1. <showcase.netins.net/web/alsmusic/jokes>

Week Five — *Waffles and Spaghetti in the Bedroom*

1. Author unknown.

Week Six — *Waffles and Spaghetti in Conflict*

1. <showcase.netins.net/web/alsmusic/jokes>

Week Seven — *Waffles and Spaghetti Achieving Together*
1. Author unknown.

Week Eight — *Waffles and Spaghetti at Home*
1. Author unknown.

Week Nine — *Waffles and Spaghetti As Parents*
1. <waycoolweddings.com> Submitted by Bruce McMahon.

2. For more on parenting, Pam Farrel, *The Treasure Inside Your Child* (Eugene, OR: Harvest House Publishers, 2000).

Week Ten — *Waffles and Spaghetti Meeting Each Other's Key Needs*
1. <waycoolweddings.com>

For more resources to enhance your relationships and build marriages or to connect with Pam and Bill Farrel for a speaking engagement, contact:

Masterful Living
629 S Rancho Sante Fe #306
San Marcos, CA 92069
(760) 727-9122

www.Masterfulliving.com
Email: mliving@webcc.net

Be sure to ask about
Men Are Like Waffles—Women Are Like Spaghetti
Video Series

Great for individual couples or groups

Other Books by Bill and Pam Farrel

Men Are Like Waffles–Women Are Like Spaghetti
Bill and Pam Farrel

Men keep life's elements in separate boxes; women intertwine everything. Providing biblical insights, sound research, and humorous anecdotes, the Farrels explore gender differences and preferences and how they can strengthen relationships.

The Treasure Inside Your Child
Pam Farrel

One of the greatest desires parents have is to prepare their children to transition successfully into adult life. In this book Pam shares tips and techniques from nearly 18 years of parenting that will build your children's confidence as you help them discover the unique gifts God has put inside them.

A Woman God Can Use
Pam Farrel

Sharing stories and insights on God's desires for us, Pam helps women sense His approval. Readers will discover how to please God, focus creativity and enthusiasm, and live lives based on biblical truth.

Other Harvest House Reading

The Power of a Praying® Wife
Stormie Omartian

Stormie Omartian shares how wives can develop a deeper relationship with their husbands by praying for them. This book is packed with practical advice on praying for specific areas, including decision-making, fears, spiritual strength, and sexuality.

The Power of a Praying® Husband
Stormie Omartian

In *The Power of a Praying® Husband* you'll find the excitement and hope that come from inviting the God who hears and answers prayer into your marriage. Even in situations full of hurt, He can do far *beyond* what you imagine—He can do the impossible!

A Marriage Without Regrets
Kay Arthur

Speaking candidly about her failed first marriage, her conversion to Christianity, and her current marriage, Kay offers practical, biblical advice on communication, significance, and parenting. She also covers God's guidelines for divorce and remarriage.